Breathing Under Water: Spirituality and the Twelve Steps
Franciscan priest and prolific author Rohr is a perfect writer on
the subject of the 12 Steps. He understands how radical a change
they bring about, and that the 12 Step program is preeminent-
ly spiritual. His easy-to-read book is essentially a commentary
on each of the steps, with twelve chapters and a postscript that
concisely tackles the big religious question of human suffering,
suffering with which addicts and their families are intimately acquainted. Jesus, Rohr answers, is no stranger to suffering.... This
is a good book for those in recovery from addiction and those who
love them.

—*Publishers Weekly*

Eager to Love: The Alternative Way of Francis of Assisi
In *Eager to Love*, [Rohr] reclaims the mysticism inherent in the
Franciscan legacy and he offers it as an alternative to the hierar-
chical, patriarchal and authoritarian Christianity that he suggests
has primary responsibility for so much of contemporary agnos-
ticism in the West.... He claims to want to "reignite the Franciscan revolution," which is universally accessible and inclusive,
offering healing and liberation. As such, he is building a bridge
between the Christian mystical tradition and estranged seekers of
every ilk.... *Eager to Love* is neither a biography of Francis nor a
history of the Franciscan order, but Rohr's reflections on the best
aspects of the Franciscan heritage as lived out by its founder and
its early worthies—Clare, Bonaventure and Dun Scotus.

—*National Catholic Reporter*

Breathing Under Water
Companion Journal

RICHARD ROHR

Originally published in the United States of America in 2015
by Franciscan Media, Cincinnati, Ohio

First published in Great Britain in 2016

Society for Promoting Christian Knowledge
36 Causton Street
London SW1P 4ST
www.spck.org.uk

Scripture quotations are the author's own paraphrase, or his choice from several
translations, particularly *The Jerusalem Bible*, published and copyright © 1966, 1967
and 1968 by Darton, Longman & Todd Ltd and Doubleday, a division of
Random House, Inc., and used by permission.

British Library Cataloguing-in-Publication Data
A catalogue record for this book is available from the British Library

ISBN 978–0–281–07514–0
eBook ISBN 978–0–281–07515–7

Typeset by Graphicraft Limited, Hong Kong
First printed in Great Britain by Ashford Colour Press
Subsequently digitally printed in Great Britain

eBook by Graphicraft Limited, Hong Kong

Produced on paper from sustainable forests

CONTENTS

Richard Rohr is a globally recognized Catholic and Christian teacher focusing on mystical and transformational traditions and is the founder and director of the Center for Action and Contemplation in Albuquerque, New Mexico, home of the Rohr Institute. He is the author of more than twenty books, including *Yes, And... Daily Meditations*; *Silent Compassion: Finding God in Contemplation*; *Immortal Diamond: The Search for Our True Self*; *Eager to Love: The Alternative Way of Francis of Assisi*; and *Breathing Under Water: Spirituality and the Twelve Steps.*

"I did not come for the healthy, but for those who need a doctor."
—Jesus (Luke 5:31)

"You see, alcohol in Latin is *spiritus* and you can
use the same word for the highest religious experience as well as for the most depraving poison."
—Carl Jung's letter to Bill Wilson in 1961, shortly before
Jung's death

"Breathing Under Water,"
Carol Bieleck, R.S.C.J.
I built my house by the sea. Not on the sands, mind
you; not on the shifting sand. And I built it of rock.
A strong house by a strong sea.
And we got well acquainted, the sea and I. Good neighbors.
Not that we spoke much. We met in silences.
Respectful, keeping our distance,
but looking our thoughts across the fence of
sand. Always, the fence of sand our barrier,
always, the sand between.

And then one day,
—and I still don't know how it happened— the sea came.
Without warning. Without welcome, even

Not sudden and swift, but a shifting across the sand like wine,
less like the flow of water than the flow of blood. Slow, but coming.
Slow, but flowing like an open wound.
And I thought of flight and I thought of

drowning and I thought of death.
And while I thought the sea crept higher, till it reached my door.
And I knew then, there was neither flight, not death, nor drowning.
That when the sea comes calling you stop being good neighbors
Well acquainted, friendly-at-a-distance, neighbors
And you give your house for a coral castle,
And you learn to breathe underwater.

I was very much surprised by the continuing response to my original 1989 audio set called *Breathing Under Water*, and later very challenged when Franciscan Media asked me to put some of these ideas into book form (2011), but then both astounded and gratified when the response only deepened and widened after its publication. Many of us began to recognize that what we once imagined was a small category of "addicted" people, was really all of us. Only the nature of the addiction changed from person to person.

My work over twenty-five years in teaching contemplative prayer and practice to many people in many cultures has made me deeply aware that there is one universal addiction that all of us suffer from: we are all addicted to ourselves. Already the early Desert Fathers and Mothers had discovered that human beings are universally addicted to *their* way of thinking which they take as natural, inevitable, and "Doesn't everybody process ideas the same way as I do?" Doesn't everybody "feel" as I do? The Buddhists and many psychologists called this *unrecognized but constant self-referencing* — quite simply ego or egotism.

Jesus, with a quite unique but striking metaphor said that "this single grain of wheat had to fall on the ground and die," or it would never bear much fruit (John 12:24). You really cannot explain that one away! Yet we did, and largely made the Christian religion, and most religion, about dressing up and dignifying our single and particular grain of wheat. No talk of practical, daily dying is allowed!

Each in our own way, we are all breathing, or trying to breathe, while not recognizing that we are first of all "underwater"—under the water of our own untested assumptions, our cultural blindness, the compulsive neurological responses often inherited from family and childhood, our early wounding (which somehow seems to be universal), and the narcissism of our own egoic responses to almost everything, including most especially our learned defenses to that early wounding—which are almost entirely unconscious and well-practiced by now.

It is the beginnings of enlightenment to begin to see this and to begin to raise our periscope above the water level. Only then might we see and find pure air to actually breathe in and out. Some might call it the air of the Spirit.

As long as you stay "underwater" you will not breathe, but you will drown instead—while not calling it drowning but presume it is "living." Most peoples' initial level of free response is very limited. While thinking they are surely "doing their own thing," they are almost totally programmed, conditioned, and addicted to everybody else's thing and everybody else's wounding *It is the foundational work of spirituality to increase, deepen, and expand your true inner freedom* (see Galatians 5:1), so you can maturely *act* and not just re-act.

It was the spiritual genius of Bill Wilson, Doctor Bob, their circle of admitted addicts, and the influence of many of the key ideas of the "Oxford Group" from 1919–1939 that all coalesced to an astounding epiphany among a group of sincere seekers toward the end of that period. It became the practical Twelve Step program in, of all places, Akron, Ohio—probably because the depth of the suffering and addiction had become "unmanageable" for so many at that time. For me, it is clearly a work of the Holy Spirit, precisely because of the coming together of so many forces, ideas, and key people without any single person or one single idea steering the insights. Like the first Pentecost, it was a descent of many tongues of fire and many tongues of speech (Acts 2:1–13) in Akron, Ohio.

For me, part of the genius of the Twelve Step program is that it combines very deep and rather obvious Scriptural principles (although not obvious till someone tells you!), a Jesuit and Catholic sense of the discernment of spirits (1 Corinthians 12:10), much hard-earned pastoral wisdom, good psychology on how people change, along with a kind of American pragmatism and practicality that has now moved it all over the world with continuing but quiet success. This feels like Gospel.

I am especially gratified that the book, and now surely this wonderful study guide created by the hard and creative work of others, seems to be largely spreading by word of mouth and not by any media blitz or merchandizing strategy. This work is especially used by those who work in jails, prisons, and rehab programs, and beyond denominational or faith boundaries, or with those who enjoy book study groups. This study guide is made-to-order for all of them.

I have every hope that this program and guide will help many precisely because it begins where the Gospel and honest psychological change begin—by the sharing of human vulnerability and human pain. Not by ideology, ideas from above, mere theories, or mere theology. Its starting place is not an abstract salvation theory but a concrete recognition of human suffering, how much of it is self-generated, and *our desire to be in solidarity with the suffering of others* (instead of adding to it by accusation), and thus to spiritually learn from one another. Peer preaching you might call it, although it does not usually feel like preaching at all.

For too long we have made the starting place "sin" in the Christian world, spent an awful lot of time trying to convince already shamed people of how shameful they indeed were. What a waste of time and God's mercy! The vast majority just tried to hide, run, or deny. We all know it is true—read the statistics. This is our postmodern, Western world, which only runs to even more addictions and farther from so much organized religion to lessen the irrational suffering, when, as Pope Francis said, the Church was meant to be "a field hospital on the edge of the battleground." If so, maybe the Twelve-Step program is the field manual and the triage guidebook for Christian life.

When the suffering becomes as great and as evident as it is in our world and in our country today, we have almost no place left to hide and every place left to heal.

This feels like *Gospel hope and Spirit generated desire*. I think it surely is.

Easter Sunday, 2015
Center for Action and Contemplation
Albuquerque, New Mexico

The quotes selected here offer nuggets of wisdom from *Breathing Under Water*. If you read the book a number of years ago, it will remind you of the key points. If you haven't yet read the book, it will be an introduction to Fr. Richard's thoughts on this topic. Reading or rereading the book after working with the companion journal will give you a deeper engagement with the text. You may want to read the chapter in the book as you work through the questions and exercises included here.

The beginning of each chapter gives the relevant step from the Twelve Steps and a selection of passages from the Hebrew and Christian Scriptures. Refer back to these while you are working through the material. They are reminders of the central theme of each chapter and how it fits into both the Christian tradition and the Twelve Step program.

At the end of each chapter, "Breathing Lessons" give you the opportunity to work through several activities that will make the message of the chapter a deeper part of your daily life.

CHAPTER ONE

Powerlessness

"Like a weaver, you roll up my life, and cut
it from the loom. From dawn to night you
are watching my failure. I cry aloud until the
morning, but like a lion you crush all my bones.
I twitter like a swallow, I moan like a dove."
—ISAIAH 38:12–14

"I cannot understand my own behavior. I
fail to carry out the very things I want to
do, and find myself doing the very things
I hate…for although the will to do what is
good is in me, the performance is not."
—ROMANS 7:15,18

"And when Jesus looked at the crowds, he felt
sorry for them, because they were harassed and
dejected, like sheep without a shepherd."
—MATTHEW 9:36

"We admitted
we were
powerless over
alcohol—that
our lives
had become
unmanage-
able."

—STEP
ONE
of the
TWELVE
STEPS

We are all spiritually powerless, however, and not just those physically addicted to a substance. Alcoholics just have their powerlessness visible for all to see. The rest of us disguise it in different ways, and overcompensate for our more hidden and subtle addictions and attachments, especially our addiction to our way of thinking.

How do you feel about being powerless? When have you experienced being powerless in your everyday life? How have you been taught to regard power and powerlessness? Spend some time writing your immediate reactions to the words *powerful* and *powerless*.

_____

_____

_____

_____

_____

_____

_____

_____

_____

_____

_____

People who have moved from seeming success
to seeming success seldom understand success
at all, except a very limited version of their own.
People who fail to do it right, by even their own
definition of right, are those who often break
through to enlightenment and compassion.

When were you surprised by something good coming out of a seeming failure? Think of a time when you got exactly what you thought you wanted and were disappointed? Why do you think that happened? How might it look different now as you look back on it with a different perspective?

_____

_____

_____

_____

_____

_____

_____

_____

_____

_____

It is God's greatest surprise and God's constant disguise, but you only know it to be true by going through it and coming out the other side yourself. You cannot know it by just going to church, reading Scriptures, or listening to someone else talk about it, even if you agree with them.

Reflect on a dark or difficult time in your past. How was God present or absent at that time? How does it look now? Write about how the memory of that time might be helpful in future situations.

_____

_____

_____

_____

_____

_____

_____

_____

_____

_____

_____

_____

_____

_____

Until you bottom out, and come to the limits of your own fuel supply, there is no reason for you to switch to a higher octane of fuel. For that is what is happening! Why would you? You will not learn to actively draw upon  *a Larger Source until your usual resources are depleted and revealed as wanting. In fact, you will not even know there is a Larger Source until your own sources and resources fail you.*

How much do you depend on your own strength and abilities to get through your everyday struggles? How easy is it for you to ask others for help? When did you last ask God for help? Name at least one area where you feel like you might be reaching "the limits of your own fuel supply."

_____

_____

_____

_____

_____

_____

_____

_____

_____

An ego response is always an inadequate or even wrong response to the moment. It will not deepen or broaden life, love, or inner laughter. Your ego self is always attached to mere externals, since it has no inner substance itself. The ego defines itself by its attachments and revulsions. The soul does not attach nor does it hate; it desires and loves and lets go. Please think about that, it can change your very notion of religion.

What area of your life do you have a need to control? How hard do you work at maintaining that control? What is it costing you in terms of physical and emotional health? How does your need to control affect your relationships?

_____

_____

_____

_____

_____

_____

_____

_____

_____

_____

_____

What the ego hates more than anything else in the world is to change—even when the present situation is not working or is horrible. Instead, we do more and more of what does not work, as many others have rightly said about addicts,  *and, I would say, about all of us. The reason we do anything one more time is because the last time did not really satisfy us deeply.*

What is your first response to a change in your life? How do you find your way to acceptance? Write about a time when you knew that you needed to make a change but resisted. Write about another time when you found something better. What are you afraid to change right now? How can you take one step forward?

_____

_____

_____

_____

_____

_____

_____

_____

_____

_____

_____

Breathing Lessons

Think about your breathing. Inhale. Exhale. Hold your breath for 20 seconds. Breathe deeply. Feel yourself relax. Think about an experience of being under water and not being able to breathe.

By definition, you can never see or handle what you are addicted to. It is always "hidden" and disguised as something else. As Jesus did with the demon at Gerasa, someone must say, "What is your name?" (Luke 8:30). The problem must be correctly named before the demon can be exorcised. You cannot heal what you do not first acknowledge.

As we begin to see the need for recovery, we have an inkling of what our addictions might be. Find an image of something that you think might be the problem. Put it someplace where it can remind you of the work you may need to do.

We suffer to get well.
We surrender to win.
We die to live.
We give it away to keep it.

Spend some time reflecting on these central paradoxes. Choose one to carry with you through the day. You might want to write it on a piece of paper, send it to yourself as a text message or email, or simply memorize it and repeat it when you have a few moments to yourself.

CHAPTER TWO
Desperate Desiring

"The God of old is still your refuge. This
God has everlasting arms that can
drive out the enemy before you."
—DEUTERONOMY 33:27

"Yes, we are carrying our own death warrant with
us, but it is teaching us not to rely on ourselves, but
on a God whose task is to raise the dead to life."
—2 CORINTHIANS 1:9

"While he was still a long way off, the father saw
him and was moved with pity. He ran to the boy,
clasped him in his arms and kissed him tenderly."
—LUKE 15:21

"Came to
believe that a
Power greater
than ourselves
could restore
us to sanity."

—STEP
TWO
of the
TWELVE
STEPS

The surrender of faith does not happen in one moment but is an extended journey, a trust walk, a gradual letting go, unlearning, and handing over. No one does it on the first or even second try. Desire and longing must be significantly deepened and broadened.

Write about a significant moment on your journey of faith to this point. Who did you have to trust in that moment? Another person? God? Yourself?

_____

_____

_____

_____

_____

_____

_____

_____

_____

_____

_____

_____

_____

To finally surrender ourselves to healing, we have to have three spaces opened up within us—and all at the same time: our opinionated head, our closed-down heart, and our defensive and defended body. That is the work of  *spirituality—and it is work. Yes, it is finally the work of "a Power greater than ourselves," and it will lead to great luminosity and depth of seeing.*

Where do you instinctively make decisions—your head, heart, or gut? Which do you consider the most trustworthy? Which do you most distrust? Imagine a dialogue with one of these three areas of your being. What would it tell you about your need to be more open?

_____

_____

_____

_____

_____

_____

_____

_____

_____

We need to be in right relationship with people, so that other people can love us and touch us at deeper levels, and so we can love and touch them. Nothing else opens up the heart space in such a positive and ongoing way.

Fr. Richard writes, "To keep the heart space open, we need some healing in regard to our carried hurts from the past." This is when we know that the work we need to do is going to take us places we might not want to go. Write about an experience of letting go of a hurt. Then write about a hurt from the past that you still carry. Reflect on the differences and similarities of the two situations.

_____

_____

_____

_____

_____

_____

_____

_____

_____

_____

_____

That is the rub of any conversion experience: You only know how much you needed it when you are on the other side! That is why you need the tenacity of faith and hope to carry you across to most transformational experiences.

When you can let others actually influence you and change you, your heart space is open.

Write about a time when someone stayed with you through a difficult time. How did their faith in you carry you through the darkness? Give thanks for those people who have helped you in the past. When were you able to carry someone else through a crisis?

_____

_____

_____

_____

_____

_____

_____

_____

_____

_____

Your heart needs to be broken, and broken open, at least once to have a heart at all or to have a heart for others.

When has your heart been broken? How has this led you to greater compassion?

_____

_____

_____

_____

_____

_____

_____

_____

_____

_____

_____

_____

_____

_____

_____

To keep our bodies less defended…is also the work of healing of past hurts and the many memories that seem to store themselves in the body. The body seems to never stop offering its messages; but fortunately, the body never lies, even though the mind will deceive you constantly.

How do you carry stress in your body? Spend some time listening to the various place in your body that hurt. Ask your body what message it's trying to communicate to you.

_____

_____

_____

_____

_____

_____

_____

_____

_____

_____

_____

_____

_____

All we can do is keep out of the way, note, and weep over our defensive behaviors, keep our various centers from closing down—and the Presence that is surely the Highest Power is then obvious, all embracing, and immediately effective.

How do you get in the way of your own healing and growth? Name three of your defensive behaviors. What can you do to begin to change at least one? What helps you stay open to life?

_____

_____

_____

_____

_____

_____

_____

_____

_____

_____

_____

_____

_____

_____

Breathing Lessons

Make this passage from Paul's Letter to the Thessalonians the centerpiece of your prayer time for the next week. Find a creative way to keep it with you through the day. "May the God of peace make you whole and holy, may you be kept safe in body, heart, and mind, and thus ready for the presence. God has called you and will not fail you" (1 Thessalonians 5:23).

The heart space is often opened by "right brain" activities such as music, art, dance, nature, fasting, poetry, games, life-affirming sexuality, and, of course, the art of relationship itself. Choose one of these activities and find a way to explore it more deeply over the next week.

Find a way to be especially good to your body this week. This will manifest itself in different ways for different people. It might mean focusing on eating healthy—or allowing yourself some delicious treat. It might be a good workout—or a long, hot bath.

CHAPTER THREE
Sweet Surrender

"O, come to the water all you who are thirsty.
Though you have no money, come! Buy corn
without money, and eat; and, at no cost, wine
and milk. Why spend money on what is not
bread, your wages on what fails to satisfy?"
—ISAIAH 55:1–2

"Work for your salvation in fear and trembling.
It is God, for his own loving purposes, who
puts both the will and the action into you."
—PHILIPPIANS 2:12–13

"Ask, and it will be given to you; search and you
will find; knock, and the door will be opened to
you. For the one who asks always receives; the
one who searches always finds; the one who
knocks will always have the door opened."
—MATTHEW 7:7–8

"Made a
decision to
turn our will
and our lives
over to the
care of God as
we understood
God."

—STEP
THREE
of the
TWELVE
STEPS

Acceptance is not our mode nearly as much as aggression, resistance, fight, or flight. None of them achieve the deep and lasting results of true acceptance and peaceful surrender. It becomes the strangest and strongest kind of power. You see, surrender is not "giving up," as we tend to think, nearly as much as it is a "giving to" the moment, the event, the person, and the situation.

Fr. Richard writes, "Surrender will always feel like dying, and yet it is the necessary path to liberation." Write about what the word *surrender* conjures up in your mind and heart. How is this influenced by your personal experiences? How is it influenced by society's perspective?

_____

_____

_____

_____

_____

_____

_____

_____

_____

_____

How long it takes each of us to just accept—to accept what is, to accept ourselves, others, the past, our own mistakes, and the imperfection and idiosyncrasies of almost everything.

What do you find difficult to accept about yourself? About people close to you? Write about whether this seems more or less difficult as you grow older.

_____

_____

_____

_____

_____

_____

_____

_____

_____

_____

_____

_____

_____

We each have our inner program for happiness, our plans by which we can be secure, esteemed, and in control, and are blissfully unaware that these cannot work for us in the long haul—without our becoming more and more control freaks ourselves. Something has to break our primary addiction, which is to our own power and our false programs for happiness.

Have you ever had the experience of turning your life over to God? What happened? Write about the experience, giving some thought to how it looks now that you're on the other side of the event.

_____

_____

_____

_____

_____

_____

_____

_____

_____

_____

_____

_____

"If anyone wants to follow me, let him renounce himself [or herself!]" (Mark 8:34, Luke 9:23, Matthew 16:4). Have we ever really heard that? It is clear in all of the Gospels: "Renouncing the self!" What could Jesus possibly mean or intend by such absolute and irresponsible language?

Spend some time reading and reflecting on Mark 8:34-37. This is a familiar passage, but sometimes we don't hear it because it frightens us. Write your first reaction and then write through that reaction to a place of greater understanding and acceptance.

_____

_____

_____

_____

_____

_____

_____

_____

_____

_____

_____

The absolute genius of the Twelve Steps is that it refuses to bless and reward what looks like any moral worthiness game or mere heroic willpower.

Fr. Richard writes. "So much that is un-love and non-love, and even manipulative "love," cannot be seen or addressed because it is so dang sacrificial. Your hands are well tied." How do you handle situations when you sense that you're being manipulated by someone else's "goodness"? How do you feel when someone calls your bluff for making sacrifices that only serve to make you look noble and heroic?

_____

_____

_____

_____

_____

_____

_____

_____

_____

_____

_____

We can only live inside the flow of forgiveness if we have stood under the constant waterfall of needed forgiveness ourselves. Only hour-by-hour gratitude is strong enough to overcome all temptations to resentment.

Write about a time when you were forgiven for something you did. How did that feel? Then write about a time when you forgave someone else. Was there any connection between the two experiences? Could you make a connection between either one and a future experience of forgiveness?

_____

_____

_____

_____

_____

_____

_____

_____

_____

_____

_____

As my father, St. Francis, put it, when the heart is pure, "Love responds to Love alone" and has little to do with duty, obligation, requirement, or heroic anything. It is easy to surrender when you know that nothing but Love and Mercy is on the other side.

How have you known unconditional love?

_____

_____

_____

_____

_____

_____

_____

_____

_____

_____

_____

_____

Breathing Lessons

Fr. Richard writes, "We have been graced for a truly sweet surrender, if we can radically accept being radically accepted—for nothing! 'Or grace would not be grace at all'! (Romans  11:6)." Spend some time writing about your experiences of being accepted (or not accepted) just for who you are, not for anything you've done.

Find a recording of "Amazing Grace" that you find especially moving. Listen to it prayerfully and let your heart be touched by the experiences of grace in your life.

Sometimes our problem is not with sacrifice but with the motivation for that sacrifice. If you are the sort of person who readily gives in to someone else's point of view or always puts your own needs after others, write about a time when you did this and then resented it. Ask yourself if you might be using self-sacrifice as a way to manipulate those around you.

CHAPTER FOUR

A Good Lamp

"Sacrifice gives you no pleasure, were I to
offer a holocaust, you would not have it. My
sacrifice is this broken spirit. You will never
scorn a crushed and broken heart."
—PSALM 50:16–17

"If inside you have the bitterness of jealousy, or
a selfish ambition, never make any false claims
for yourself or cover up the truth with lies."
—JAMES 3:14

"Be awake and pray that you pass the test. The
spirit is willing, but the flesh is weak."
—MATTHEW 26:41

"Made a
searching and
fearless moral
inventory of
ourselves."

—STEP
FOUR
of the
TWELVE
STEPS

Moral scrutiny is not to discover how good or bad I am and regain some moral high ground, but it is to begin some honest "shadow boxing" which is at the heart of all spiritual awakening.

Fr. Richard writes, "Yes, 'the truth will set you free' as Jesus says (John 8:32), but first it tends to make you miserable." What part of you do you not want to see? What are you afraid will happen if you're honest with yourself? Can you begin to imagine being free of that fear?

_____

_____

_____

_____

_____

_____

_____

_____

_____

_____

_____

_____

_____

Without confidence in a Greater Love, none of us will have the courage to go inside, nor should we. It merely becomes silly scrupulosity (2 Timothy 3:6) and not any mature develop-ment of conscience or social awareness.

When have you used a weakness or a failure as an excuse not to move forward? How might clinging to a surface fault keep you from looking more deeply at the ways in which you need to change?

_____

_____

_____

_____

_____

_____

_____

_____

_____

_____

_____

_____

The goal is actually not the perfect avoidance of all sin, which is not possible anyway (1 John 1:8–9, Romans 5:12), but the struggle itself, and the encounter and wisdom that comes from it.

Fr. Richard writes, "People only come to deeper consciousness by intentional struggles with contradictions, conflicts, inconsistencies, inner confusions, and what the biblical tradition calls 'sin' or moral failure." When have you struggled to face the truth? What happened?

_____

_____

_____

_____

_____

_____

_____

_____

_____

_____

_____

_____

Shadow boxing, a "searching and fearless moral inventory," is for the sake of truth and humility and generosity of spirit, not vengeance on the self or some kind of total victory over the self. Seeing and naming our actual faults is probably not so much a gift to us—although it is—as it is to those around us.

Other people can probably see our faults better than we can. Write about a time when someone criticized your behavior. Take a step back from your defensive reaction and look for the truth that may lie at the heart of that criticism. How does this help you begin an honest moral inventory?

_____

_____

_____

_____

_____

_____

_____

_____

_____

_____

_____

Your shadow self is not your evil self. It is just that part of you that you do not want to see, your unacceptable self by reason of nature, nurture, and choice. That bit of chosen blindness, or what A.A. calls denial, is what allows us to do evil and cruel things—without recognizing them as evil or cruel.

Write about a time when your unwillingness to acknowledge an inner failure or weakness led you to hurt someone else. Then write about how you might have handled the situation differently.

_____

_____

_____

_____

_____

_____

_____

_____

_____

_____

_____

_____

STEP FOUR

We absolutely need conflicts, relationship diffi-
culties, moral failures, defeats to our grandi-
osity, even seeming enemies, or we will have no
way to ever spot or track our shadow self. They
are our necessary mirrors. Isn't that sort of a
surprise? And even then, we usually catch it out of the corner of
our eye—in a graced insight and gifted moment of inner freedom.

Think of a time when you stopped denying and admitted that some situation or relationship was bad, unnecessary, or harmful. What happened?

_____

_____

_____

_____

_____

_____

_____

_____

_____

_____

The game is over once we see clearly because evil succeeds only by disguising itself as good, necessary, or helpful. No one consciously does evil. The very fact that anyone can do stupid, cruel, or destructive things shows they are at that moment unconscious and unaware. Think about that: Evil proceeds from a lack of consciousness.

Think of a time when you admitted failure. How did that experience bring personal change?

_____

_____

_____

_____

_____

_____

_____

_____

_____

_____

_____

_____

_____

The God of the Bible is best known for transmuting and transforming our very evils into our own more perfect good. God uses our sins in our own favor! God brings us—through failure—from unconsciousness to ever-deeper  *consciousness and conscience. How could that not be good news for just about everybody?*

Fr. Richard writes, "Somehow goodness is transferred by radiance, reflection, and resonance with another goodness, more than by any act of self-achievement. We do not pull ourselves up; we are pulled." Write about an experience when you knew absolutely that you were not saved by your own action or strength. How might this make you less afraid of admitting weakness?

_____

_____

_____

_____

_____

_____

_____

_____

_____

Breathing Lessons

O Lord, you have searched me and known me.
You know when I sit down and when I rise up;
*   you discern my thoughts from far away.*
You search out my path and my lying down,
and are acquainted with all my ways.

Read Psalm 139 slowly and prayerfully. Write about your feelings at being known so intimately by God.

Ongoing shadow boxing is absolutely necessary because we all have a well-denied shadow self. We all have that which we cannot see, will not see, dare not see. It would destroy our public and personal self-image.

Do some shadow boxing as a physical activity. Don't try to over-think it. Let your body lead you to the inner space where your shadow lives. What feelings arise as you move back and forth with this hidden side of yourself?

Only the soul knows that we grow best in the shadowlands. We are blinded inside of either total light or total darkness, but "the light shines on inside the darkness, and it is a light that darkness cannot overcome" (John 1:5). In darkness we find and ever long for more light.

Sit in a darkened room for a period of time, perhaps ten or fifteen minutes. Let your thoughts dwell on the darkness, on how you feel in the dark. Then light a candle. Focus on the light. Notice how it fills the space around itself and expands into the dark room. After a time, turn on a light in the room and again notice the effect of the candle's light. How does that candle represent the presence of the Light of the World?

CHAPTER FIVE

Accountability IS Sustainability

"All the time I kept silent and my bones wasted away. I groaned day in and day out, my heart grew parched as stubble in summer drought, and at last I admitted to you that I had sinned and no longer concealed my guilt."
—PSALM 32:3–5

"So confess your sins to one another, and pray for one another, and this will cure you."
—JAMES 5:16

"If you forgive others their sins, they are indeed forgiven. If you withhold forgiveness from one another, they are held bound."
—JOHN 20:23

"Admitted to God, to ourselves and to another human being the exact nature of our wrongs."

—STEP FIVE *of the* TWELVE STEPS

When human beings "admit" to one another "the exact nature of their wrongs," we invariably have a human and humanizing encounter that deeply enriches both sides—and even changes lives—often forever! It is no longer an exercise to achieve moral purity, or regain God's love, but in fact a direct encounter with God's love. It is not about punishing one side but liberating both sides.

Fr. Richard writes, "As any good therapist will tell you, you cannot heal what you do not acknowledge, and what you do not consciously acknowledge, will remain in control of you from within, festering, and destroying you and those around you." What personal failure do you find most difficult to acknowledge? How much more difficult would it be to admit that failure to someone else?

_____

_____

_____

_____

_____

_____

_____

_____

Have you ever experienced the embarrassed and red-faced look of shame and self-recognition on the face of anyone who has been loved gratuitously after they have clearly done wrong? This is the way that God seduces us all into the  *economy of grace—by loving us in spite of ourselves in the very places where we cannot or will not or dare not love ourselves.*

When did someone love you in spite of your actions? How did that make you feel? How did it make you want to be a better person?

_____

_____

_____

_____

_____

_____

_____

_____

_____

_____

_____

_____

_____

God resists our evil and conquers it with good, or how could God ask the same of us?! Think about that. God shocks and stuns us into love. God does not love us if we change, God loves us so that we can change. Only love effects true inner transformation, not duress, guilt, shunning, or social pressure. Love is not love unless it is totally free. Grace is not grace unless it is totally free.

Write about ways that people in your past may have used shame or guilt to try to make you change your behavior? How successful was it? How has that influenced your perception of God?

_____

_____

_____

_____

_____

_____

_____

_____

_____

_____

_____

Our tendency to resist, doubt, and deny ourselves forgiveness made it necessary for one person to speak and act with absolute authority for the sake of the soul: "I announce to you in the name of God, and with the authority of the Holy Spirit, that all of your sins are forgiven," the confessor might say. There often needs to be a human mirror to reflect the un-seeable divine gaze, especially if our heads and body are bowed in shame.

Fr. Richard writes, "Accountability and healing was so deemed necessary in the history of Christianity that it became an official and designated role in the community, and even a 'Sacrament.'" Write about your experiences—good and bad—of the sacrament of reconciliation through the years. How do those experiences color your approach to Step 5?

_____

_____

_____

_____

_____

_____

_____

_____

_____

Only mutual apology, healing, and forgiveness offer a sustainable future for humanity. Otherwise we are controlled by the past, individually and corporately. We all need to apologize, and we all need to forgive or this human project will surely self-destruct. No wonder that almost two-thirds of Jesus' teaching is directly or indirectly about forgiveness.

Fr. Richard writes, "What humanity needs is an honest exposure of the truth, and true accountability and responsibility for what has happened. Only then can human beings move ahead with dignity." How can you begin to stop replaying hurtful memories?

_____

_____

_____

_____

_____

_____

_____

_____

_____

_____

Breathing Lessons

If you're Catholic, make a commitment to celebrate the Sacrament of Reconciliation.

After the "searching and fearless moral inventory" of Step 4, you may have discovered some area that you could better deal with through some professional help. Explore options for finding that help and make an appointment as a first step.

Identify someone in your life who you believe can be a friend and confidante as you're working through these exercises. Ask them if they are willing and able to talk with you about these issues. Respect their answer and their boundaries.

CHAPTER SIX

The Chicken or the Egg: Which Comes First?

"This is what I shall tell my heart, and so recover hope: the favors of Yahweh are not all passed, his kindnesses are not exhausted. They are renewed every morning."
—LAMENTATIONS 3:21–22

"Not that I have become perfect yet: I have not yet won, but I am still running to capture the prize for which Christ Jesus captured me."
—Philippians 3:12

"The only thing that counts is not what humans want or try to do, but the mercy of God."
—Romans 9:16

"If I will it? Of course I will it! Be healed."
—Jesus (Luke 5:12)

"Were entirely ready to have God remove all of these defects of character."

—STEP SIX *of the* TWELVE STEPS

Step 6 manages to again talk paradoxically. It says that we must first fully own and admit that we have "defects of character," but then equally, step back and do nothing about it, as it were, until we are "entirely ready" to let God do the job!

When have you had an experience of letting go and letting God? When did you get in God's way, believing that you had a better answer?

_____

_____

_____

_____

_____

_____

_____

_____

_____

_____

_____

_____

_____

_____

I like to say that we must "undergo God." Yes, God is pure and free gift, but there is a necessary undergoing to surrender to this Momentous Encounter. As others have put it, and it works well in English, to fully understand is always to  *stand under and let things have their way with you. It is strangely a giving up of control to receive a free gift and find a new kind of "control." Try it and you will believe the paradox for yourself.*

Write about your fears if you let go of control and allow God to change you. What might be the source of those fears?

_____

_____

_____

_____

_____

_____

_____

_____

_____

_____

_____

So the waiting, the preparing of the mind for "chance," the softening of the heart, the deepening of expectation and desire, the "readiness" to really let go, the recognition that I really do not want to let go, the actual willingness to change is the work of weeks, months, and years of "fear and trembling."

Are you more comfortable with acting or waiting? What happens if you approach a problem from a stance opposite the one you normally prefer?

_____

_____

_____

_____

_____

_____

_____

_____

_____

_____

_____

_____

_____

But the recognition that it is finally "done unto me" is the supreme insight of the Gospels, which is here taught practically in Step 6. It is the same prayer of Mary at the beginning of her journey (Luke 1:38) and of Jesus at the end of his life (Luke 23:46): "Let it be done unto me!"

Fr. Richard writes, "Struggle with the paradox itself, hold the creative tension until you can see that two seeming contraries might not be contrary at all. I suggest that you find examples of how this has been true in your own life, and surely in any journey toward sobriety." Write your response.

_____

_____

_____

_____

_____

_____

_____

_____

_____

_____

_____

By personal temperament you will start on one side or the other, but finally you must build the bridge between the two—and let it be built for you—both at the same time. Or to reverse an old aphorism: We must pray as if it all depends on us, and work as if it all depends on God.

Fr. Richard writes, "It seems we must both surrender and take responsibility." How does this quotation express itself in the ability to dance with a partner? What does this analogy have to say about recovery from addictions?

_____

_____

_____

_____

_____

_____

_____

_____

_____

_____

_____

_____

Breathing Lessons

It is no surprise at all that our common metaphors for the Holy Spirit all honor and point to a kind of flow experience: living water, blowing wind, descending flames, and alighting doves.

What is your favorite metaphor for the Holy Spirit? Pair that image with your need to let go of some character defect. Spend some time reflecting on it in prayer. Then find a creative way (writing, visual arts, dance) to express what you've discovered. Find a way to keep this image present as you move forward on your journey.

Sit in a comfortable chair with your hands relaxed in your lap, palms facing up. Breathe in and out slowly and deeply several times. Pray Mary's words, "Let it be done to me according to your word." Continue to focus on your breathing. Notice how this prayer makes you feel.

CHAPTER SEVEN

Why Do We Need to Ask?

"Have mercy on me, O God, in your goodness, in your great tenderness wipe away
all my faults, wash me clean of my guilt,
and purify me from all my sin."
—PSALM 51:1–2

"If there is anything you need, pray for it, asking
God for it with thanksgiving; and the peace of
God, which is much greater than understanding,
will guard both your thoughts and your heart."
—PHILIPPIANS 4:6–7

"In your prayers do not babble on as the
pagans do, for they think that by using many
words they will make themselves heard. Do
not be like them; your Father knows what
you need even before you ask him."
—MATTHEW 6:7–8

> "Humbly
> asked [God]
> to remove our
> shortcomings."
>
> —STEP
> SEVEN
> *of the*
> TWELVE
> STEPS

We ask not to change God but to change ourselves. We pray to form a living relationship, not to get things done. Prayer is a symbiotic relationship with life and with God, a synergy that creates a result larger than the exchange itself.

Fr. Richard writes, "Prayer is not a way to try to control God, or even get what we want. As he says in Luke's Gospel the answer to every prayer is one, the same, and the best: the Holy Spirit! (See 11:13.) God gives us power more than answers." How have your prayers changed throughout your life? How are prayer and grace linked? How would you describe grace?

_____

_____

_____

_____

_____

_____

_____

_____

_____

_____

_____

The death of any relationship with anybody is to have a sense of entitlement. Any notion that "I deserve," "I am owed," "I have a right to," "I am higher than you" absolutely undermines any notion of faith, hope, or love between the involved parties. To undo and undercut this arrogant and soul-destructive attitude, Jesus told us all to stay in the position of a beggar, a petitioner, a radical dependent, which is always spiritually true, if we are honest.

Fr. Richard writes, "We are all and forever beggars before God and the universe." What does it mean to you to be radically dependent? Do you find it difficult to ask for help? What are some areas in your life where you have a sense of entitlement? What would happen if you reversed that attitude?

_____

_____

_____

_____

_____

_____

_____

_____

Our life situation and our style of relating to others is "the truth" that we actually take with us to the grave. It is who we are, more than our theories about this or that. Jesus says as much in his parable of the two sons. (See Matthew 21:28–32.) Prayers of intercession or petition are ways of situating your life within total honesty and structural truth.

What is your experience with prayer of petition? What are your expectations of the "result"?

_____

_____

_____

_____

_____

_____

_____

_____

_____

_____

_____

_____

_____

_____

Step 7 says that we must "humbly ask God to remove our shortcomings." Don't dare go after your faults yourselves or you will go after the wrong thing, or more commonly a clever substitute for the real thing. "If you try to pull out

the weeds, you might pull out the wheat along with it," as Jesus says (Matthew 13:29).

When have you changed something in your life, only to discover that the change made things worse instead of better? How might you have avoided that mistake? What can you do to be more careful in the future?

_____

_____

_____

_____

_____

_____

_____

_____

_____

_____

_____

You have to let God (1) reveal your real faults to you (usually by failing and falling many times!), and then (2) allow God to remove those faults from his side and in God's way. If you go after them with an angry stick, you will soon be left with just an angry stick—and the same faults at a deeper level of disguise and denial.

When have you tried to eliminate a fault, only to have it reappear later? How might you be more patient with yourself and your faults? How can you begin to see failure as an opportunity to grow?

_____

_____

_____

_____

_____

_____

_____

_____

_____

_____

_____

_____

Life is a gift, totally given to you without cost, every day of it, and every part of it. A daily and chosen "attitude of gratitude" will keep your hands open to expect that life, allow that life, and receive life at ever-deeper levels of satisfaction—but never to think you deserve it. *Those who live with such open and humble hands receive life's "gifts, full measure, pressed down, shaken together, and running over into their lap"* (Luke 6:38).

Fr. Richard writes, "In my experience, if you are not radically grateful every day, resentment always takes over. For some reason, to ask 'for your daily bread' is to know that it is being given. To not ask is to take your own efforts, needs, and goals—and yourself—far too seriously. Consider if that is not true in your own life." What will it take to see everything as gift and be grateful with your life?

_____

_____

_____

_____

_____

_____

_____

_____

After a few years in recovery, you will know that your deep and insatiable desiring came from God all along, you went on a bit of detour, looked for love in all the wrong places, and now have found what you really wanted anyway. God is willing to wait for that.

Write about something you desired in the past (or the present!) and think about how it reflects in some way your deeper desire for God. If the reflecting is muddied or obscured, how might you find greater clarity?

_____

_____

_____

_____

_____

_____

_____

_____

_____

_____

_____

Breathing Lessons

Prayers of petition are perhaps our most common prayer from the desperate plea of "Help!" to prayer of intercession for those we love and those who are in grave need. Write about times when you have prayed for someone or something. How was that prayer answered?

Start to keep a "gratitude journal." Each day, write several things for which you are grateful. Notice how easy or difficult this is for you, and whether that changes from day to day depending on the circumstances of your life. After you have done this for a few weeks, write about whether you notice any change in your attitude or outlook on life.

God's totally positive and lasting way of removing our short-comings is to fill up the hole with something much better, more luminous, and more satisfying. Then your old shortcomings are not driven away, or pushed underground, as much as they are exposed and starved for the false program for happiness that they are. Like used scaffolding, our sins fall away from us as unneeded and unhelpful because now a new and better building has been found.

Spend some time playing with a child's set of blocks or a deck of cards or a lump of clay. Build various structures, knock them down, notice what makes a structure more or less solid and stable. As you move the pieces around, think about how they represent different aspects of your life, your relationships, your strengths and weaknesses.

CHAPTER EIGHT

Payback Time

"Nathan said to David, 'You are the man!...' And David said to Nathan, "I have indeed sinned."
—2 SAMUEL 12:7, 13

"In judging others you condemn yourself, since you behave no differently than those you judge."
—ROMANS 2:1

"If you are bringing your gift to the altar, and there remember that your brother or sister has anything against you, go first and be reconciled to him or her, and then come back and present your gift."
—MATTHEW 5:23–24

"Made a list of all persons we had harmed, and became willing to make amends to them all."

—STEP EIGHT *of the* TWELVE STEPS

God fully forgives us, but the "karma" of our mistakes remains, and we must still go back and repair the bonds that we have broken. Otherwise others will not be able to forgive us, will remain stuck, and we will both remain a wounded world. We usually need to make amends to even forgive ourselves.

Fr. Richard writes, "When you move to higher states of love and transformation, you do not jump over the earlier stages but must go back and rectify the earlier wrongs, or there will be no healing or open future for you—or for those you have hurt." Write about some significant times in your past when you have hurt or failed someone. Begin to think about ways you can repair the damage that was done.

_____

_____

_____

_____

_____

_____

_____

_____

"Amazing grace" is not a way to avoid honest human relationships, but to redo them—but now gracefully—for the liberation of both sides. Nothing just goes away in the spiritual world; all must be reconciled and accounted for.

What relationship would you like to redo? Write about things you did wrong, things you might have done differently? What change can you make today?

_____

_____

_____

_____

_____

_____

_____

_____

_____

_____

_____

_____

_____

You learn to salve the wounds of others by knowing and remembering how much it hurts to hurt. Often this memory comes from the realization of your past smallness and immaturity, your selfishness, your false victimhood, and your cruel victimization of others. It is often painful to recall or admit, yet this is also the grace of lamenting and grieving over how we have hurt others.

When have you been hurt by someone who failed to apologize or make amends in any way? Write about the experience and let yourself truly feel the pain of it. Now recall someone you may have hurt. How does this move you toward apologizing?

_____

_____

_____

_____

_____

_____

_____

_____

_____

_____

_____

Our family, friends, and enemies, however, are not as kind or patient as God. They need a clear accounting to be free and go ahead with their lives. Often they just need to talk it through, hear your understanding, and maybe your  *sincere apology. Usually they need to offer their understanding of the situation and how it hurt them. Neither side needs to accuse or defend, but just state the facts as we remember them, and be open to hear what the other needed, heard, or felt.*

Part of being willing to make amends is being able to see the hurt from both sides. It can be difficult to listen to other people's experience of the effects of our actions. Spend some time reflecting on how someone might have perceived your actions in the past.

_____

_____

_____

_____

_____

_____

_____

_____

_____

Step 8 is quite programmed, concrete, and specific. "Make a list," it says, and that list is of "all those we have harmed." Note that it does not say those who have harmed us, which will just get us back into the self-serving victim role. The plan is absolutely inspired here, and knows that it needs to push the addict out of his or her immense selfishness.

As you reflect on those you may have hurt in the past, how often do you fall into the trap of making excuses based on their behavior toward you? What can you do to avoid this trap? How difficult is it to be honest about these relationships and your own responsibility?

_____

_____

_____

_____

_____

_____

_____

_____

_____

_____

The second bit of spiritual genius in Step 8 is that it recognizes how long it might take to be truly "willing." It even uses the active verb "became willing to make amends to them all" to help us see that it is always a process and must finally include all. To offer an apology in a way that can actually heal the other takes wisdom and respect for the other.

Fr. Richard writes, "We all need to do some clean-up work inside. For humans, there is only a slow softening of the heart, a gradual lessening of our attachment to our hurts, our victimhood as a past identity, or any need to punish or humiliate others." Keep in mind that this step is more about having internal conversations about your own role in past conflicts. Only when you have come to some peace with your own hurts can you reach out to others. Write honestly about your feelings as you look back at a troubled relationships. What hurts do you choose to hold on to?

_____

_____

_____

_____

_____

_____

_____

Remember Einstein's brilliant idea that no problem can be solved by the same consciousness that caused the problem in the first place. Making such a list will change your foundational consciousness from one of feeding resentments to a mind that is both grateful and humble—all the time.

Who is that one person you find most difficult to forgive? What can you do to want to ask for forgiveness and receive it?

_____

_____

_____

_____

_____

_____

_____

_____

_____

_____

_____

_____

_____

Breathing Lessons

Make a list of people who have hurt you in the past. With each one, feel the hurt that may still linger in your heart. Then hold each person in prayer. Place the person and the hurt you feel  in God's hands. Slowly tear the list into small pieces as a sign that you're willing to let go of the hurt.

"Instead of making lists of who hurt me, I now make lists of people I have perhaps hurt, failed, or mistreated, and then do something about it. It might be a note, a call, a visit, a meaningful gift, an invitation, an outright apology. God will show you the best way, the best place, the best time, and the best words. Wait and pray for them all."

Make a list of people you have hurt in the past. As you write the names, hold each person in prayer. Reflect on the list of actions Fr. Richard suggests and choose an appropriate one for each person on the list.

CHAPTER NINE

Skillful Means

"Like apples of gold in a silver setting is
a word that is aptly spoken. It is a golden
ring, an ornament of finest gold, such is
a wise apology to an attentive ear."
— PROVERBS 25:11–12

"To listen to the word and not obey it is like
looking at your own features in a mirror and
then, after a quick look, going off and immediately forgetting what you look like."
— JAMES 1:23

"Father, I have sinned against heaven and against
you. I no longer deserve to be called your
son, treat me as one of your paid servants."
— LUKE 15:19

"Made direct
amends to
such people
wherever
possible,
except when
to do so would
injure them
or others."

— STEP
NINE
of the
TWELVE
STEPS

Jesus invariably physically touched people and met people when he healed them. It is face-to-face encounters, although usually difficult after a hurt, that do the most good in the long run, even if the other party rebuffs you at the first attempt. You opened the door from your side, and it thus remains open, unless you reclose it.

Fr. Richard writes, "Step 9 is telling us how to use skillful means to both protect our own humanity and to liberate the humanity of others. It also says that our amends to others should be 'direct,' that is, specific, personal, and concrete, in other words, probably not an email or a tweet." How comfortable are you having difficult conversations face to face?

_____

_____

_____

_____

_____

_____

_____

_____

_____

_____

But the most skillful insight is the cleverly added "except when to do so would injure them or others." Bill W could only have learned such wisdom by doing it wrong, probably many times.

Write about a time when someone rebuffed your attempt to apologize. Write about a time when waiting to apologize paid off. Reflect on the difference and similarities in the two situations.

_____

_____

_____

_____

_____

_____

_____

_____

_____

_____

_____

_____

If not done skillfully, an apology can actually make the problem and the hurt worse, and the Twelve Steps were experienced enough to know that. Not everything needs to be told to everybody, all the time, and in full detail. Sometime it only increases the hurt, the problem, and the person's inability to forgive. This all takes wise discernment and often sought-out advice from others.

Who has been an elder, a wise mentor, in your life? How has his or her advice helped you in difficult situations? How might it help you discern and clarify your approach to Step 9?

_____

_____

_____

_____

_____

_____

_____

_____

_____

_____

What people want to hear in salacious and gossipy detail has now been fed by our media-saturated society, and our wanting to know has become our right to know. Gossip is not a right but a major obstacle to human love and spiritual wisdom. Paul lists it equally with the much more grievous "hot sins" (Romans 1:29–31), and yet most of us do it rather easily.

Fr. Richard writes, "We have a myth of 'total disclosure' in our culture that is not always fair or even helpful. Just because it is factually true, does not mean everyone can handle it or even needs to handle it, or has a right to the information. You need to pray and discern about what the other needs to hear and also has the right to hear." Write about a situation in your life where you need to heed this advice. Be honest about your motives in revealing personal details to others.

_____

_____

_____

_____

_____

_____

_____

_____

Skillful means is not just to make amends but to make amends in ways that "do not injure others." Truth is not just factual truth (the great mistake of fundamentalists), but a combination of both text and context, style and intent. Our supposed right to know every "truth" about our neighbor too often feeds those with pre-existing malice, bias, or mental imbalance, and leads to spin, distortion, and misinterpretation of supposed facts.

Our lives are never completely our own. Write about the ways in which some of the deepest truths of your life have an impact on other people. Reflect on how to respect their privacy as well as your own as you go through a program of recovery.

_____

_____

_____

_____

_____

_____

_____

_____

_____

_____

The Twelve Steps are about two things: making amends and keeping us from wounding one another further. Too much earnest zeal here, "spilling the beans" on everybody's lap, will usually create a whole new set of problems.
Many people simply do not have the proper "filters" to know how to process ideas or information; they often misuse it without intending to misuse it. Even sincere people can do a lot of damage with information that they are not prepared to handle, and often make rash judgments that are not true or helpful.

When did you act too hastily to correct a mistake? What happened?

_____

_____

_____

_____

_____

_____

_____

_____

_____

_____

Breathing Lessons

Look at the list you made in chapter eight of people you have harmed. For each person on the list, prayerfully reflect on whether making amends for that hurt would be in his or her best interest. If you are unable to make direct amends, make a special effort to hold that person in prayer on a regular basis. If there is some direct action you can take, commit to doing that.

For a week or two, notice how much of the news and social media is concerned with the private lives of celebrities and even ordinary people. Reflect on how you encourage that sort of coverage by your attention and your willingness to comment and gossip in your own circle of acquaintances. Take time to ask yourself if this makes you feel more or less secure and why that might be the case. Then ask yourself if it makes you feel more or less willing to be open about your own life in an appropriate way.

CHAPTER TEN

Is This Overkill?

"But who can detect his own failings? Who
can expose his own hidden faults?"
—PSALM 19:12

"Even pagans who never heard of the law, can be
said to 'be' the law; it is engraved on their hearts.
They can call forth this witness, their own inner
mental dialogue of accusation and defense."
—ROMANS 2:14–15

"Then Jesus said to him a third time, 'Simon, son
of John, do you love me?' Peter was upset that
he asked him a third time, and said, "Lord, you
know everything, you know that I love you."
—JOHN 21:17

"Continued to
take personal
inventory
and when we
were wrong
promptly
admitted it."

—STEP
TEN
of the
TWELVE
STEPS

Consciousness is the subtle and all-embracing mystery within and between Everything. It is like the air we breathe, take for granted, and do not appreciate. Consciousness is not the seeing but that which sees me seeing. It is not the knower but that which knows that I am knowing. It is not the observer but that which underlies and observes me observing.

Fr. Richard writes, "You must step back from your compulsiveness, and your attachment to yourself, to be truly conscious. Consciousness cannot be 'just me' because it can watch 'me' from a distance." What are some ways you can begin to be conscious?

_____

_____

_____

_____

_____

_____

_____

_____

_____

_____

For the properly detached person (read "non-addicted"), deeper consciousness comes rather naturally. They discover their own soul—which is their deepest self—and yet has access to a Larger Knowing beyond themselves.

Fr. Richard writes, "Meister Eckhart said detachment was the whole deal, and the early Franciscans seemed to talk about nothing else, which they called 'poverty.'" How does detachment help you to separate yourself from your feelings, thoughts, and compulsive patterns of perception?

_____

_____

_____

_____

_____

_____

_____

_____

_____

_____

_____

On one level soul, consciousness, and the Holy Spirit can well be thought of as the same thing, and it is always larger then me, shared, and even eternal. That's what Jesus means when he speaks of "giving" us the Spirit or sharing his consciousness with us.

How does the Holy Spirit act in your life as a Divine Guide and Teacher?

Wisely, Step 10 does not emphasize a moral inventory, which becomes too self-absorbed and self-critical, but it speaks of a "personal inventory." In other words, just watch yourself objectively, calmly, and compassionately.  *You will be able to do this from your new viewing platform and perspective as a grounded child of God.*

Set aside some time to look calmly and objectively at your life in this present moment: the good and the bad, the contentment and the stress, the grace and the struggles. Write about what you observe. If it helps you to stay detached, write about yourself in the third person, using your name instead of "I."

"The Spirit will help you in your weakness" (Romans 8:26). From this most positive and dignified position you can let go of, and even easily "admit your wrongs." You are being held so strongly and so deeply that you can stop holding onto, or defending, yourself. God forever sees and loves Christ in you; it is only we who doubt our divine identity as children of God.

Fr. Richard writes, "You now have an implanted position and power whereby you can see yourself calmly and compassionately without endless digging, labeling, judging, or the rancor that we usually have toward our own imperfection." How does seeing yourself as a beloved child of God help you to look honestly at your life?

_____

_____

_____

_____

_____

_____

_____

_____

_____

Don't judge, just look can be your motto —
and now with the very eyes of God. That will
awaken consciousness, and then things will
usually take care of themselves, with even the
least bit of honesty and courage.

Fr. Richard writes, "When you are standing in your inherent dignity, you can easily do Step 10, calmly taking 'the personal inventory,' and then having the security to 'promptly admit it when you are wrong.' People who know who they are find it the easiest to know who they aren't." How much reflection time do you need to admit when you're wrong or you've made a mistake? How has that time shortened over the last weeks or months as you have begun working this program?

_____

_____

_____

_____

_____

_____

_____

_____

_____

Whenever you do anything stupid, cruel, evil, or destructive to yourself or others, you are at that moment unconscious, and unconscious of your identity. If you were fully conscious, you would never do it. Loving people are always highly conscious people. To rely on any drug or substance is to become unconscious.

When is a time that evil won out in your life? What has changed to lead you to good?

_____

_____

_____

_____

_____

_____

_____

_____

_____

_____

_____

_____

Breathing Lessons

*To be fully conscious would be to love every-
thing on some level and in some way—even
your mistakes. To love is to fall into full
consciousness, which is contemplative, non-*

*dualistic, and including everything—even "the last enemy to be
destroyed, which is death itself" (1 Corinthians 15:26). That is
why we must, absolutely must, love!*

Write about the person or persons who have shown you most deeply
what it means to love and be loved. Reflect on how they show you
the face of the God who is love. Reach out to them in some way to
let them know how grateful you are for their presence in your life.
Spend some time exploring the Examen of St. Ignatius:

Become aware of God's presence.
Review the day with gratitude.
Pay attention to your emotions.
Choose one feature of the day and pray from it.
Look toward tomorrow.

If you find this helpful in doing Step 10, resolve to make it part of
your daily routine.

CHAPTER ELEVEN

An Alternative Mind

"Be still, and know that I am God."
— PSALM 46:10

"You must put aside your old self which has been corrupted by following illusory desires. Your mind must be renewed by a spiritual revolution."
— EPHESIANS 4:22–23

"In the morning, long before dawn, he got up, left the house, and went off to a lonely place to pray."
— MARK 1:35

"Sought through prayer and meditation to improve our conscious contact with God, as we understood [God], praying only for knowledge of [God's] will for us and the power to carry that out."

— STEP
ELEVEN
of the
TWELVE
STEPS

It is work to learn how to pray, largely the work of emptying the mind and filling the heart. That is all of prayer in one concise and truthful phrase! At early-stage praying, there has usually been no real "renouncing" of the small and passing self (Mark 8:34), so it is not yet the infinite prayer of the Great Body of Christ, but the very finite prayer of a small "body" that is trying to win, succeed, and take control— with a little help from a Friend. God cannot directly answer such prayers, because frankly, they are usually for the wrong thing and from the wrong self, although we do not know that yet.

How has learning to be more honest with yourself changed the way you pray?

_____

_____

_____

_____

_____

_____

_____

_____

_____

_____

If you are able to switch minds to the mind of Christ, your prayer has already been answered! That new mind knows, understands, accepts, and sees correctly, widely, and wisely. Its prayers are always answered because they are, in fact, the prayers of God too.

Fr. Richard writes, "In short, prayer is not about changing God, but being willing to let God change us, or as Step 11 says, 'praying only for the knowledge of his will.'" When did you pray for something that you didn't get? As you look back on it, how was God's plan better than what you thought you needed? Write about your experience of "unanswered prayers."

_____

_____

_____

_____

_____

_____

_____

_____

_____

_____

_____

True prayer is always about getting the "who" right. Who is doing the praying? You or God in you? Little you or the Christ Consciousness? The contemplative mind prays from a different sense of Who–I–am. It rests, and abides in the Great I AM, and draws its life from the Larger Vine (John 15:4–5), the Deeper Well (John 4:10–14).

Write about your growing into an experience of praying with the mind of Christ.

_____

_____

_____

_____

_____

_____

_____

_____

_____

_____

_____

_____

_____

It is the prayer of quiet and self-surrender that will best allow us to follow Step 11, which Bill W must have recognized by also using the word meditation, when that word was not common in Christian circles at all at that time. And he was right, because only contemplative prayer or meditation invades, touches, and heals the unconscious! This is where all the garbage lies—but also where God hides and reveals "in that secret place" (Matthew 6:6).

Spend some time in meditation, perhaps focusing only on a few words from Scripture or your favorite name for God. Write about any realizations you have about the experience.

_____

_____

_____

_____

_____

_____

_____

_____

_____

_____

_____

The Twelve Step Program was quite ahead of its time in recognizing that we need forms of prayer and meditation that would lead us to "conscious contact with God" beyond mere repetition of correct titles and names and formulas, which religions fight about ("God as we understand God."). Such a Step 11 can lead us to real inner "knowledge of his will for us" (instead of just external commandments for all), and for the "power to carry it out" (actual inner empowerment and new motivation from a deeper Source).

Write about your understanding of God or a Higher Power. How has it changed for you over the years? How does it compare to what you have been taught?

_____

_____

_____

_____

_____

_____

_____

_____

_____

_____

Peoples' willingness to find God in their own struggle with life—and let it change them—is their deepest and truest obedience to God's eternal will. We must admit this is what all of us do anyway, as "God comes to us disguised as our life"! Remember, always remember, that the heartfelt desire to do the will of God is, in fact, the truest will of God. At that point, God has won, and the ego has lost, and your prayer has already been answered.

What do you think of when people refer to "God's will"? How can you deepen your understanding of that phrase?

_____

_____

_____

_____

_____

_____

_____

_____

_____

_____

Breathing Lessons

Over the next few weeks, explore a variety of prayer forms, both familiar and new. Spend enough time with each one to get a good sense of whether it resonates with your life at this time. Then select one or two and make time for them in your daily and weekly routine. Revisit this exercise from time to time as your life and spiritual needs change.

Explore a prayer form from a religious tradition that is different than your own. This can be a good way to break out of the doldrums of routine prayer.

CHAPTER TWELVE
What Comes Around Must Go Around

"You have cured me and given me life, my suffering has turned to health. It is you who have kept my soul from the pit of nothingness, you have thrust all my sins behind your back! The living, the living are the ones who praise you, as I do today."
—ISAIAH 38:16–17, 19

"What we have heard and known for ourselves must not be withheld from our descendants, but be handed on by us to the next generation."
—PSALM 78:3–4

"Simon, Simon, you must be sifted like wheat, and once you have recovered, you in your turn must strengthen your brothers."
—LUKE 22:31–32

"What was given to you freely, you must give away freely."
—MATTHEW 10:8

> "Having had a spiritual awakening as a result of these steps, we tried to carry this message to alcoholics, and to practice these principles in all our affairs."
>
> —STEP TWELVE *of the* TWELVE STEPS

It is a karmic law of in and out, and what Jesus really meant when he sent the disciples out "to cast out devils, and to cure all kinds of diseases and sickness" (Matthew 10:1) or to "Go out to the world and proclaim the Gospel to all creation" (Mark 16:16). He knew you had to hand the message over before you really understood it or could appreciate it yourself.

Fr. Richard writes, "You do not truly comprehend any spiritual thing until you yourself give it away. Spiritual gifts increase only by 'using' them, whereas material gifts normally decrease by usage." When have you taught someone something and wound up learning more than you taught? How can you share what you've learned here with someone else?

_____

_____

_____

_____

_____

_____

_____

_____

_____

_____

We now return to where it should all start—the necessity of "a vital spiritual experience" or what Step 12 calls a spiritual awakening. It is the grand plan and program for human deliverance. Yes, God could have created us already awakened, but then we would have been mere robots or clones. If God has revealed anything about who God is, then it is enormously clear that God loves and respects freedom—to the final and full and riskiest degree.

How is knowledge gained through experience more a part of you than something you've only heard from someone else? How has your sense of the spiritual life grown through the journal work you have done here? What have you learned from making mistakes and starting over, falling and getting up again?

_____

_____

_____

_____

_____

_____

_____

_____

_____

A good spirituality achieves two huge things simultaneously: It keeps God absolutely free, and not bound by any of our formulas, and it keeps us utterly free ourselves and not forced or constrained by any circumstances whatsoever, even human laws, sin, limitations, failure, or tragedy.

How does God's gift of free will make you appreciate all the experiences in your life, the good and the bad?

_____

_____

_____

_____

_____

_____

_____

_____

_____

_____

_____

_____

_____

_____

Again and again, you must choose to fall into a love that is greater with both friends and children. It is all training for the falling into The Love that is the Greatest. All loves are a school of love, and their own kind of vital spiritual experience—until a lasting Relationship with the Real finally takes over. You learn how to "fall in love" by falling many times, and you learn from many fallings how also to recover from the falling. How else would you? But best of all, you only know what love is by falling into it, almost against your will, because it is too scary and too big to be searched out, manufactured, or even imagined ahead of time.

Fr. Richard writes, "The only way to be delivered from our "body of death" is a love that is greater, a deeper connection that absorbs all the negativity and irritation with life and with ourselves. Until we have found our own ground and connection to the Whole, we are all unsettled and grouchy." Write about an experience of being "unsettled and grouchy." What were the circumstances? How did you react? What pulled you out of that mood? What are the great loves in your life that can help you through such times?

_____

_____

_____

_____

_____

Over time, the addict is forced to "up the ante" when the fix does not work. You need more and more of anything that does not work. If something is really working for you, then less and less will satisfy you. On my good days, a grasshopper can convert me.

What do you think about more than anything else? Could this be a "god"? The Twelve Steps, like any conversion, is an ongoing process. How do you feel about having to go back to Step 1?

_____

_____

_____

_____

_____

_____

_____

_____

_____

_____

_____

_____

_____

_____

Breathing Lessons

With these twelve important breathing lessons, you now know for yourself that you can breathe, and even breathe under water. Because the breath of God is everywhere.

What is the most significant thing you have learned about yourself in the process of working through this companion journal? Write about the experience and commit to an ongoing process of self-reflection and working the 12 steps.

How can you gently encourage others to begin to explore the hidden depths of their own lives? Remember that this kind of journey can only be undertaken freely and willingly.

If you uncovered problems with an addiction that already has an established 12-Step program, you might want to consider finding a group and going to meetings as a way to continue the exploration you have begun here.

AN UNEXPECTED POSTSCRIPT
Only a Suffering God Can Save

Who among those who have read the Gospels does not
know that Christ makes all human suffering his own?
—ORIGEN, *On Prayer*

Only if we are not alone in this universe, can I tolerate my aloneness. Only if there is a bigger and better outcome, can I calm down and begin to listen and look. Only if human suffering is first of all and last of all divine suffering can I begin to connect any dots. If we are joining God, and God is joining us, in something greater than the sum of all its parts, can I find a way through all of this.

Fr. Richard writes, "Deep communion and dear compassion is formed much more by shared pain than by shared pleasure. I do not know why that is true." How does your own experience show you the truth of this insight? Write about a time when shared suffering brought you closer to someone? How do you feel about God sharing your suffering?

_____

_____

_____

_____

_____

_____

_____

_____

_____

Only those who have tried to breathe under water know how important breathing really is, and will never take it for granted again. They are the ones who do not take shipwreck or drowning lightly, they are the ones who can  name *"healing" correctly, they are the ones who know what they have been saved from, and the only ones who develop the patience and humility to ask the right questions of God and of themselves.*

When have you received advice from someone who had clearly never been through a similar experience? How did that make you feel? Write about a time when someone was able to reach out to you with compassion because they had suffered a similar pain. Reflect on the differences between the two.

_____

_____

_____

_____

_____

_____

_____

_____

Those who have passed over eventually find a much bigger world of endurance, meaning, hope, self-esteem, deeper and true desire, but most especially, a bottomless pool of love both within and without. Their treasure hunt is over, and they are home, and home free!

Write about this journey through your hidden depths as though it were a treasure hunt. What were some clues? What were some obstacles? What did you discover at the end of the path?

_____

_____

_____

_____

_____

_____

_____

_____

_____

_____

_____

_____

_____

_____

It is at precisely this point that the suffering God and a suffering soul can meet. It is at this point that human suffering makes spiritual sense, not to the rational mind, the logical mind, or even the "just and fair" mind, but to  *the logic of the soul, which I would state in this way: Suffering people can love and trust a suffering God. Only a suffering God can "save" suffering people. Those who have passed across this chasm can and will save one another.*

Write about an experience of deep pain and suffering. What do you recall of your emotions at the time? What have you come to realize now that you have come through to the other side? How can this make you a more compassionate fellow traveler?

_____

_____

_____

_____

_____

_____

_____

_____

_____

The suffering creatures of this world have a Being who does not judge or condemn them, or in any way stand aloof from their plight, but a Being who hangs with them and flows through them, and even toward them in their despair. How utterly different from all the greedy and bloodthirsty gods of most of world history! What else could save the world? What else would the human heart love and desire?

Write about a time when you felt as though you were being judged and condemned by someone who didn't understand what you were going through. Have you ever imagined God as this kind of judge? How does Jesus in the Gospels, and especially in his passion and death, offer a different reality?

_____

_____

_____

_____

_____

_____

_____

_____

_____

To mourn for one is to mourn for all. To mourn with all is to fully participate at the very foundation of Being Itself. For some reason, which I am yet to understand, beauty hurts. Suffering opens the channel through which all of Life

flows and by which all creation breathes, and I still do not know why. Yet it is somehow beautiful, even if it is a sad and tragic beauty.

Write about a time when you saw a glimpse of great beauty in the midst of a tragic experience. Did it startle you at the time? How have you come to understand it?

_____

_____

_____

_____

_____

_____

_____

_____

_____

_____

_____

Breathing Lessons

What humiliated and wounded addict cannot look on the image of the crucified Jesus and see himself or herself? Who would not rush toward surrender and communion with such a crucified God, who against all expectations, shares in our powerlessness, our failure, and our indignity? Who would not find himself revealed, renamed, and released inside of such a God?

Spend some time reflecting on an image of the crucified Christ. You might want to explore several until you find one that resonates with your own experience. Write about your reaction to the suffering he endured.

You see, only the survivors know the full terror of the passage, the arms that held them through it all, and the power of the obstacles that were overcome. All they can do is thank God they made it through! For all the rest of us it is mere speculation, salvation theories, and "theology."

Think about stories you've read about people who have survived some sort of natural disaster. You might want to look for some online accounts. As you ponder their experience, let memories of your own close calls (actual or metaphorical) surface.

There is no shortage of suffering in the world around us. Find a cause that resonates with you and reach out in whatever ways you can to help alleviate some of that suffering. In this way, you can participate in God's saving grace and pass on to others the gift you yourself have received.